Earth's Changing
Islands

by Neil Morris

Raintree

Chicago, Illinois

© Copyright 2004 Raintree
Published by Raintree, a division of Reed Elsevier, Inc.
Chicago, IL 60602
Customer Service 888-363-4266
Visit our website at www.raintreelibrary.com

For more information address the publisher
Raintree, 100 N. LaSalle, Suite 1200, Chicago IL 60602

Printed and bound in China by South China Printing Company
07 06 05 04 03
10 9 8 7 6 5 4 3 2 1

Editorial: Keith Ulrich
Design: Erica Barraca
Picture Services: Michelle Lisseter and Bridge Creative Ltd
Illustrations: Bridge Creative Services Ltd
Production: Sal D'Amico

Cover photograph of North Male Atoll, Fauholhu Fushi, Maldives, reproduced with permission of Pictures Colour Library.

The publishers would like to thank
Margaret Mackintosh for her assistance
in the preparation of this book.

Library of Congress Cataloging-in-Publication Data

Morris, Neil, 1946-
  Earth's changing islands / Neil Morris.
     p. cm. -- (Landscapes and people)
Summary: Looks at the geography and people that make up island regions throughout the world, focusing on the changing characteristics of both.
Includes bibliographical references (p.   ) and index.
ISBN 1-4109-0177-7 (hc), 1-4109-0344-3 (pb)
 1. Islands--Juvenile literature. 2. Landscape changes--Juvenile literature. 3. Island ecology--Juvenile literature. 4. Nature--Effect of human beings on--Juvenile literature. [1. Islands. 2. Landscape changes. 3. Island ecology. 4. Ecology. 5. Nature--Effect of human beings on.] I. Title. II. Series: Morris, Neil, 1946-   . Landscapes and people.
GB471.M66 2003
910'.914'2--dc21

                              2003002149

Acknowledgments
The publishers would like to thank the following for permission to reproduce photographs:
p. 7 Michael St. Maur Sheil/Corbis, p.12 NASA/Corbis, p. 13 Owaki-Kulla/Corbis, p. 16 Tim Thompson/Corbis, p. 18 Gail Mooney/Corbis, p. 21 Macduff Everton/Corbis, p. 23 Jose F. Poblete/Corbis, p. 25 Jan Butchofsky-Houser/Corbis, p. 27 Richard Klune/Corbis; p. 11 C Dani-l Jeske/Natural Science Photos, p. 14 Pete Oxford/Natural Science Photos, p. 24 Ben Stobart/Natural Science Photos; p. 17 Any Rouse/NHPA; p. 5 Scott Winer/Oxford Scientific Films, p. 6 Tony Martin/Oxford Scientific Films, p. 9 Hjalmar Bardarson/Oxford Scientific Films, p. 15 Robin Bush/Oxford Scientific Films.

Contents

What Is an Island?   4

How Are Islands Formed?   6

Changing Life   14

Changing Settlements   18

Changing Islands   24

Island Facts and Figures   28

Glossary   30

Further Reading   31

Index   32

Any words appearing in the text in bold, **like this,** are explained in the Glossary.

What Is an Island?

What do you think of when you think of an island? Does it have sandy beaches and warm blue seas? Or is it a cold, rocky place battered by ocean waves and the wind? Whichever one you think of, you're right. An island can be both of these things, and many others, too.

An island is a piece of land that is completely surrounded by water. The biggest islands are in the world's oceans and seas. Many smaller islands can be found in lakes and rivers. Very small islands are called **islets.**

Greenland is the biggest island in the world. It lies between the North Atlantic and Arctic Oceans, off the coast of North America.

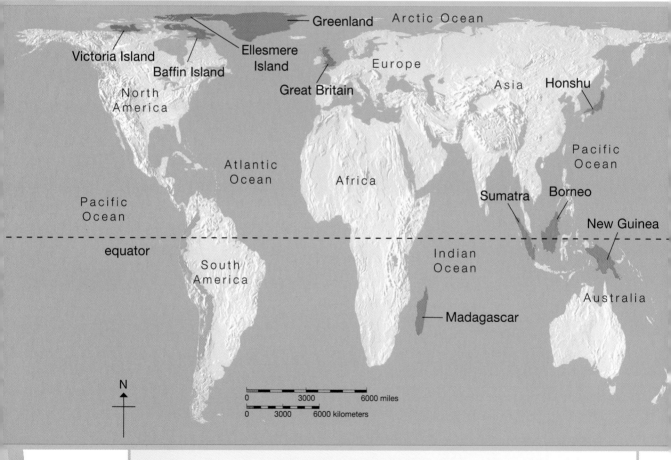

This world map shows the location of the ten biggest islands (in red). Three of them—New Guinea, Borneo, and Honshu— lie in the world's largest ocean, the Pacific.

The huge land masses of Australia and Antarctica are also surrounded by water, so they are really massive islands. They are so big, though, that people call them **continents.**

Changing islands

There are many different kinds of islands, and they were formed in different ways. Some were made by **erupting volcanoes.** Others were formed from the skeletons of dead sea creatures. These islands are home to millions of amazing animals and plants, some of which are found nowhere else. People also live on, use, and change islands. In recent years **tourists** have had a great effect on many of the world's smaller islands. In some places this has brought problems, which you will read about later in this book.

● *Islands are pieces of land that are completely surrounded by water. This is one of the many small islands that make up the country of Fiji, in the Pacific Ocean.*

World of islands

There are islands all over the world. Some, such as Madagascar, off the coast of Africa, form a separate country. Other islands are part of another country. Sumatra, for example, belongs to Indonesia. When islands are grouped closely together, they form a cluster called an **archipelago.** Japan is an archipelago made up of four large islands and hundreds of small islets.

How Are Islands Formed?

Islands may look like any other land, but they are all really the tops of hills or mountains that rise above sea level. The rest of the hill or mountain is under water and makes up the **seabed.** Islands change slowly over many years. The way that islands change depends on how they were formed.

Continental islands

Islands that are close to a much larger mass of land are called **continental** islands. The mass of land is a **continent,** also called the **mainland.** Continental islands were once connected to the mainland. Some were cut off by the movement of rocks beneath the surface of Earth. This surface is called Earth's **crust.** The crust is not one continuous layer, like the shell of an egg, but is cracked into huge pieces. We call these pieces **plates,** and though they seem still to us, they actually move very slowly. As they do so, some pieces of land break away from others, and the gap between them is filled by ocean. The large island of Madagascar, off the coast of Africa, was formed this way. The island split away tens of millions of years ago, long before there were any people living on Earth.

● Today, Greenland is almost completely covered by an ice sheet that is more than 2 miles (3,000 meters) thick in places. This was how most of northern Europe looked during the last ice age.

Melting ice

Other continental islands were cut off thousands of years ago because of changes in the sea level. The British Isles are a good example of this. They were once part of mainland Europe. More than 10,000 years ago, during the last **ice age,** huge sheets of ice stretched for thousands of miles across northern Europe. When the ice age ended, and large parts of these **ice sheets** started to melt, the extra water made the sea level rise. Water filled the low land between present-day France and England, forming the English Channel. Great Britain became an island.

Changing with the tide

Twice a day the water in the world's oceans rises and then falls again. The rising and falling are called **tides.** When water covers more land, we say that the tide has come in, or that it is "high tide." Tidal islands are pieces of land that are cut off from the mainland at high tide. Mont-Saint-Michel is surrounded by **sandbanks,** which connect the island to the coast of northern France at low tide. When the tide rises, the sandbanks are covered by water.

● *Mont-Saint-Michel is a tidal island, about 2,953 feet (900 meters) all the way around. According to legend, a French bishop was visited in a dream by an archangel, and told to build a church on the island. Its abbey was founded in 966, and the island was named after the archangel (Saint Michael in English). Today, Mont-Saint-Michel is very popular with* **tourists.**

Oceanic islands

Many of the world's islands were never connected to a **continent.** Some of them lie thousands of miles away from the **mainland.** These islands are formed by the action of underwater **volcanoes,** which occur at the edge of Earth's **plates. Lava** and ash build up on the ocean floor as the volcanoes **erupt.** This forms a mountain, which keeps growing higher until, eventually, it reaches above sea level and becomes an island. Volcanic island groups such as the Philippines and Indonesia, in southeast Asia, form in regions where one plate is forced beneath another. Some volcanic **archipelagos,** like the Aleutian Islands of Alaska, have the same curved shape as the plates where they form. These are called island arcs.

> ● *Mauna Loa, on the island of Hawaii, is the world's largest active volcano. Nearby Mauna Kea is 113 feet (36 meters) higher but has not erupted for many years. A smaller active volcano is called Kilauea. Another, called Loihi, is growing underwater to the south, and will eventually become an island.*

HAWAIIAN ISLANDS

Kauai

Niihau

Oahu

Honolulu

Molokai

N

Lanai

Maui

Haleakala

Kahoolawe

North America

Hawaiian Islands

Pacific Ocean

Mauna Kea

Mauna Loa

Kilauea

Hawaii

Loihi

0   30   60 miles
0   30   60 kilometers   ● volcano

Over the hot spot

The islands of Hawaii lie in the middle of the Pacific Ocean. They are a chain of eight main islands and many other **islets.** They were formed as the ocean floor moved very slowly over a hot area, called a **hot spot,** beneath Earth's **crust.** This hot spot spewed out very hot or **molten** rock onto the **seabed.** Over thousands of years, layers of rock built up to form an underwater mountain. Eventually the mountain poked above the ocean surface to make an individual Hawaiian island.

An island is born

One day in 1963, fishermen saw steam rising from the ocean off the coast of Iceland. At first they thought it must be smoke from a burning ship, but it was actually a volcanic island nearing the surface. By the next day, it had formed a small island, and it kept growing over the next three years. The island was called Surtsey. Seeds soon reached the island, carried there by the wind and by birds. They produced plants and, before long, seabirds were nesting among the rocks. Over the years breeding **colonies** of birds began to appear on Surtsey.

The new island off Iceland is called Surtsey. It was named after the ancient Norse god Surt, who ruled over a land of fire giants.

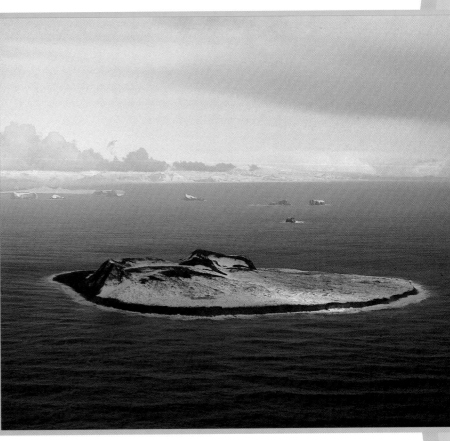

Coral islands

Coral islands form and grow in warm, shallow water. They are made of tiny, colorful sea animals. The animals are related to sea anemones and jellyfish, and are called coral polyps. Millions of these creatures live together in **colonies.** When they die, their limestone skeletons remain, and eventually become joined together. This is how coral **reefs** and islands grow. Over many years sand and soil build up on the island, so that plants can grow there. This means that people can live there, too. The Maldives in the Indian Ocean are made up of more than a thousand small coral islands. People live on more than 200 of the islands.

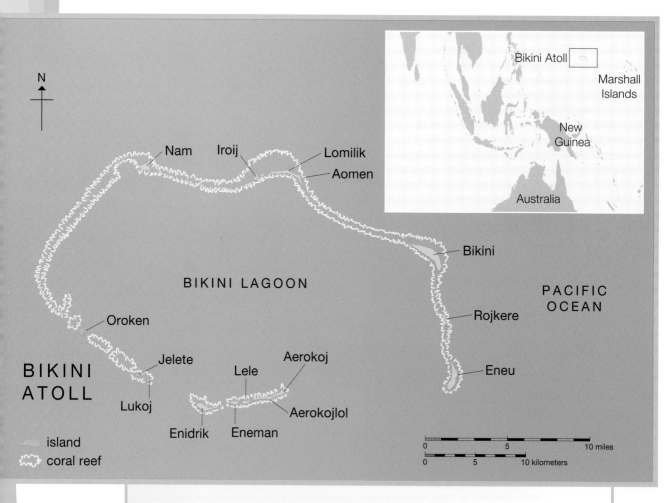

● *Bikini Atoll belongs to the Marshall Islands. Its lagoon is about 25 miles (40 kilometers) across, and its largest island is also called Bikini. From 1946 to 1958 it was used by the United States as a test site for nuclear explosions, and people living there had to move to another island.*

The Marshalls

The Marshall Islands in the central Pacific Ocean are made up of 29 **atolls** and 5 main islands. An atoll is a ring-shaped chain of coral islands. These begin as parts of a coral reef growing around a volcanic island. This is called a fringing reef. After the **volcano** has stopped **erupting,** over time it is gradually eroded (worn away). The volcanic island begins to sink and the coral forms a barrier reef. When the island has completely disappeared, the coral islands remain as an atoll. The islands surround an enclosed stretch of water called a **lagoon.**

Bora-Bora

The tropical island of Bora-Bora belongs to the Society Islands and is part of French Polynesia in the South Pacific. It pushed up from the Pacific Ocean about 3 million years ago as a volcano. A fringe of coral grew around it, and now only the tip of the volcanic mountain remains. In time, Bora-Bora will become an atoll, like Bikini.

The island at the front of the picture is part of the reef around Bora-Bora.

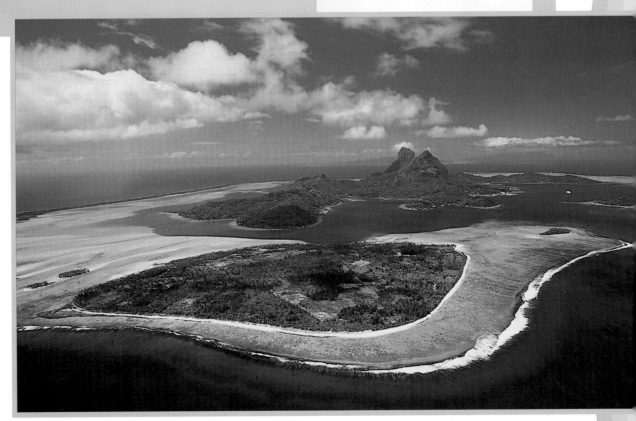

Barrier islands

Barrier islands form near shorelines. They are made up of sand, mud, and tiny stones. Ocean waves and strong winds push these materials and pile them up into a series of ridges. The ridges run parallel to the shore of the **mainland,** and they are sometimes called barrier beaches.

Barrier islands are very low, and sometimes they are covered with sand. In severe storms, waves carry huge amounts of sand over a barrier island, wearing it away on one side and building it up on the other. In this way, smaller islands can move toward the shore of the mainland over hundreds of years.

Long Beach, Long Island

Long Island (seen below from the Space Shuttle *Columbia*), off the coast of New York, is another kind of barrier island. It is made of rocks that were broken up, moved, and laid down by glaciers. At the end of the last **ice age,** the rocks formed ridges. These have been worn down over the past 10,000 years, leaving a low, hilly island that is 118 miles (190 kilometers) long. Long Island also has its own sandy barrier beaches. The best known are Fire Island and Long Beach.

Hatteras Island

There are many barrier islands on the Atlantic coast of the United States and along the gently sloping shores of the Gulf of Mexico. Hatteras Island, off the coast of North Carolina, is part of Cape Hatteras National Seashore. This coastline is known for its windswept sand dunes and **sandbanks,** which have always been very dangerous to shipping. Because of the number of shipwrecks, this region is known as the Graveyard of the Atlantic.

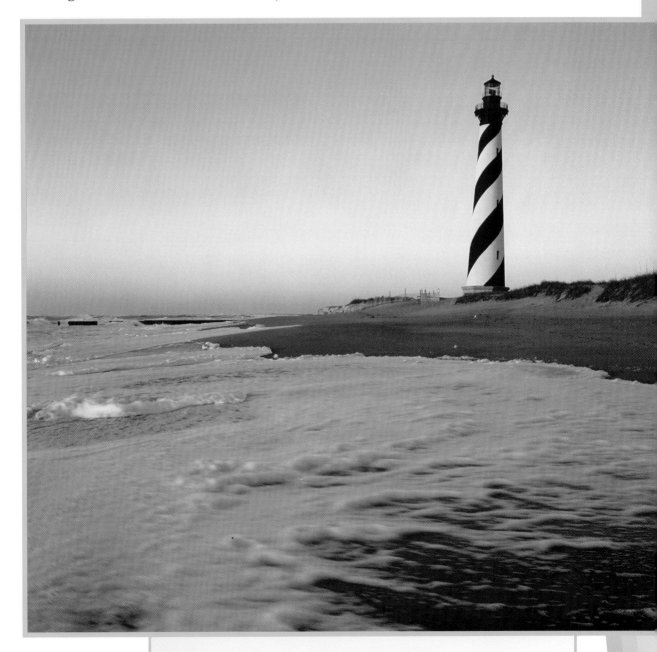

● *Boats and ships rely on Cape Hatteras Lighthouse to avoid being wrecked on the coastline.*

Changing Life

The animals and plants that live on a particular island or group of islands may be cut off from other types of wildlife. Long ago birds flew across the ocean and other animals swam to the islands. Plant seeds floated across the ocean or were carried by the wind or by birds. Storms sometimes carried animals and plants long distances. They adapted to their new surroundings and changed in ways that helped them to live on their particular island. Because of this some islands have their very own kinds of wildlife.

Madagascar

As far as its plants and animals go, the large island of Madagascar really is a world apart. Tenrecs, which look like hedgehogs, and monkey-like lemurs live only on Madagascar and the nearby Comoros islands. Two-thirds of the world's chameleons—lizards that can change color when they are angry or frightened—also live there. More than a hundred bird **species** are **unique** to Madagascar. The island has at least ten thousand different kinds of flowering plants, and three-quarters of these grow nowhere else on Earth.

In Madagascar this group of ring-tailed lemurs is sitting in the trees where they can feed on fruit, leaves, and bark. Their ringed tails are longer than their bodies.

Giant tortoises

The Galápagos Islands lie in the Pacific Ocean, about 621 miles (1,000 kilometers) from the South American **mainland.** They are home to a number of unique animals, including giant tortoises. There are several different tortoises on the islands. The largest has a shell up to 4 feet (1.2 meters) long, and weighs about 595 pounds (270 kilograms). A slightly smaller giant tortoise lives on the **coral atoll** of Aldabra, in the Seychelles islands of the Indian Ocean.

Land of the kiwi

The islands of New Zealand split away from an ancient **continent** about 80 million years ago. Large land animals never developed there, but there is one representative of the age of the dinosaurs. The tuatara is a lizard-like reptile that scientists believe is almost exactly the same as reptiles that lived about 200 million years ago, when dinosaurs roamed the earth. Tuataras still live on small islands off New Zealand. There are also two famous flightless birds that live only in New Zealand. The first is the kiwi (see photo, right), which has become the national emblem. The second is the largest parrot in the world—the kakapo, or owl parrot.

Introducing animals

In the 1800s, European settlers took many animals with them in their boats when they sailed to New Zealand. These included rabbits and weasels, which soon became pests. They damaged crops and other, smaller animals, because they had no natural enemies—except humans. The settlers also introduced English breeds of sheep, which farmers raised for their meat and wool. These are still important products for New Zealand today.

Island reserves

Small islands with no people act as natural **reserves** for animals and plants. Wildlife adapts (or changes) to the kinds of plants and smaller animals available to eat. Smaller animals, such as the flightless birds of New Zealand (see page 15), can survive if there are no large **predators** around to eat them. Animals and plants adapt to the local conditions.

On the Galápagos islands, there are more than ten different kinds of finches. Some of these songbirds live in the trees and feed on insects. Others spend most of their time on the ground, feeding on fallen seeds and fruits. Many of these island creatures would find it difficult to survive outside their **unique** environment. On many **inhabited** islands, the people have set up reserves so that the plants and animals are not disturbed.

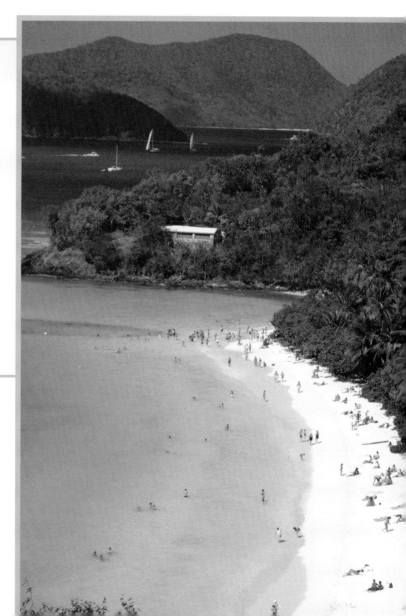

*The U.S. Virgin Islands National Park was set up in 1956. The waters surrounding the main islands are included in the park, which protect the coral **reefs** that teem with colorful tropical fish. Tourists enjoy the islands' many beaches.*

Philippine eagle

The Philippines is made up of more than 7,000 islands. Only about 900 of them are inhabited, but still some of the islands' animals are dying out because they no longer have enough space. The Philippine eagle, which is one of the world's largest birds of **prey,** likes to live in large forests. There, the eagle can find plenty of small animals to swoop down on and kill. It is one of 172 kinds of birds that live only on these islands. On the Philippines's second largest island, Mindanao, a special center has been set up to teach people about the eagles and to help protect them.

Protecting the "man of the forest"

Borneo is the world's third largest island. Its tropical climate and **rain forests** make the ideal home for the orangutan (shown below). The name of this large ape means "man of the forest" in the Malay language. Orangutans live only on Borneo and in a small region of the neighboring island of Sumatra. Because much of the Borneo rain forest is being cut down for timber, special reserves have now been set up to protect the orangutan and other large animals, such as the Asian rhinoceros.

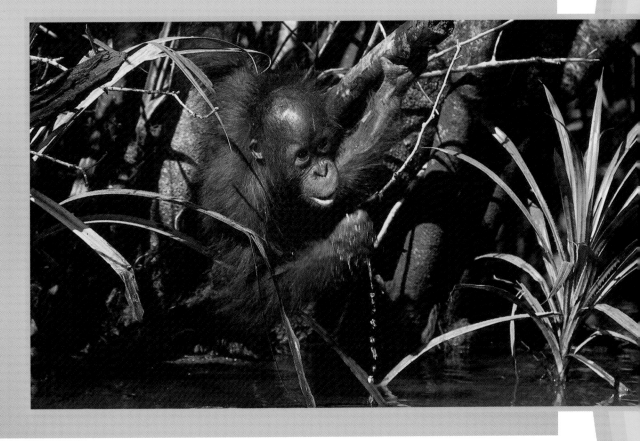

Changing Settlements

As humans began spreading out around the world, they hunted wild animals and gathered roots and berries for food. They followed rivers and coastlines, but could not visit faraway islands until they had developed oceangoing boats. This meant that many of the world's islands were the last places on Earth to be explored and settled. Some people, however, realized that islands had certain important advantages. The ocean offered protection because islands were difficult to reach.

Crete

The Minoan **civilization** developed about 4,500 years ago on the island of Crete in the Mediterranean Sea. The first people to settle in Crete probably sailed from Asia Minor (present-day Turkey) in about 7000 B.C.E. The early Cretans were farmers, growing grain and raising sheep and goats. Around 3000 B.C.E. they discovered how to make bronze. Legend says that under the rule of King Minos, they built great palaces, such as Knossos. We call these people Minoans, after their king.

The circle of islands

The Cyclades are a group of around 30 Greek islands in the Aegean Sea, to the north of Crete. The islands got their name from the Greek word for "circle," because they form a circle around the small island of Delos.

● *The Minoans built the great palace of Knossos, on the island of Crete, about 4,000 years ago. Today, you can visit the restored ruins.*

A settlement on the island of Kythnos is the earliest that has been uncovered, and may be up to 9,000 years old. The first people to settle there also came from Asia Minor.

Polynesians

The people known as Polynesians live on many small islands in the Pacific Ocean. They were the first people to live on Easter Island to the east (where they settled around 400 C.E.), Hawaii to the north (from about 600 C.E.), and New Zealand to the south (where they landed in about 1000 C.E.). Historians believe that the Polynesians sailed in oceangoing canoes from the mainland of southeast Asia.

Viking explorers

The Vikings were a great seafaring people of Scandinavia. They used islands as stepping stones to travel all the way across the Atlantic Ocean. First, they sailed in their longships from Norway to the Shetlands, north of Scotland. They went on to the Faroes, before settling in Iceland, and then Greenland. Around 1002 C.E. a Viking named Leif Ericsson sailed even further. He named the first land he and his sailors reached Helluland, meaning "land of flat stones." This was probably Baffin Island, in present-day Canada.

First people of St. Lucia

St. Lucia is an island country in the West Indies, to the east of the Caribbean Sea. Today about 150,000 people live on the island. The first people to live there were the Arawaks and Caribs, who sailed from South America. During the 1600s, the French and British arrived from Europe. Control of the island changed hands many times between these two countries until 1814, when it was officially taken over by Great Britain.

Freed slaves

By 1814 the Europeans had brought many Africans to work as slaves on sugar **plantations.** Britain banned slavery throughout its empire 20 years later. Over the next 4 years, 13,000 slaves were freed. They were joined over the next 50 years by people from Portugal and India, who came to work on the island's plantations. The British gradually allowed the islanders more control, and St. Lucia became an independent country in 1979. Today's islanders are mostly **descendants** of African slaves.

St. Lucia is a mountainous island with tropical vegetation. This map shows how its land is used. The capital, Castries, is the largest town and the main port.

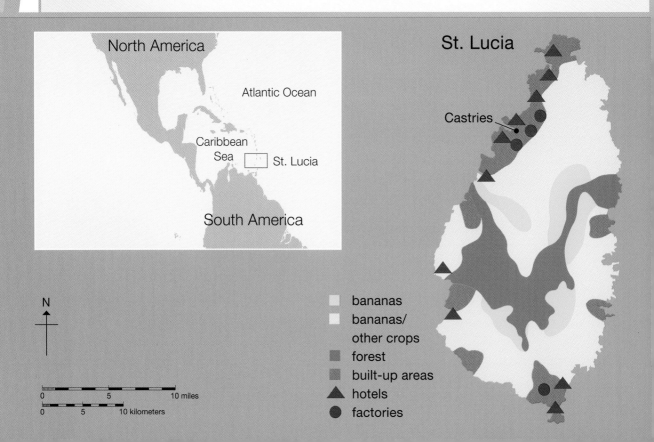

North America

Atlantic Ocean

Caribbean
Sea   St. Lucia

South America

St. Lucia

Castries

N

0   5   10 miles
0   5   10 kilometers

bananas
bananas/
other crops
forest
built-up areas
hotels
factories

Farming and industry

St. Lucia's towns lie near the coast, but more than half the islanders live in rural areas. The island's main **resource** is bananas, which make up almost half of the country's **exports.** Many of the bananas are grown on small family farms, but there are also large plantations. The islanders also export coconuts and cocoa. There are a few factories producing clothes, electrical products, paper, and textiles.

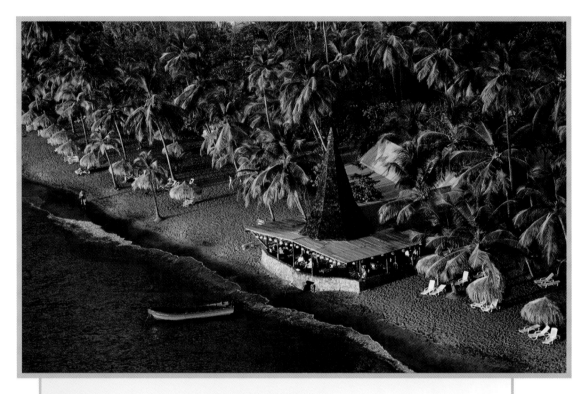

● *Vacation resorts on beautiful beaches, like this one on the coast of St. Lucia, attract tourists from all over the world.*

Tourism

Like many Caribbean islands, St. Lucia has a warm climate and |lots of sandy beaches. This makes it attractive to tourists from many parts of the world. It is a very hilly island, with **rain forest** and tropical **vegetation.** The **tourist** industry is growing quickly, and this helps provide jobs for local people, especially in hotels and restaurants. Increased tourism also brings problems for many of the islanders. As more and more land is bought up by private companies, there is less room for small farms and local communities.

The importance of islands

Islands often have great importance for the countries to which they belong. They provide harbors, which help with trade, and offer coastlines and beaches that are attractive to **tourists.** Some islands have more **territory** than their **mainland** countries. The world's biggest island, Greenland, is a **self-governing province** of Denmark. Denmark lies more than 1,864 miles (3,000 kilometers) away in Europe. Greenland is about 50 times bigger than its mainland country but has a much smaller population.

Hong Kong

Hong Kong Island lies across Victoria Harbor from Kowloon peninsula, on the southeast coast of China. The island became a British territory in 1842 after a war between China and the United Kingdom. It was agreed that the island would remain British for 99 years after 1898. Because of its natural harbor, Hong Kong grew as an important business and banking center, as well as a busy port. In 1997 Hong Kong became part of China again.

Hong Kong (which means "fragrant harbor") is the name of an island and its main city as well as a region of China. The region is made up of more than 200 islands altogether.

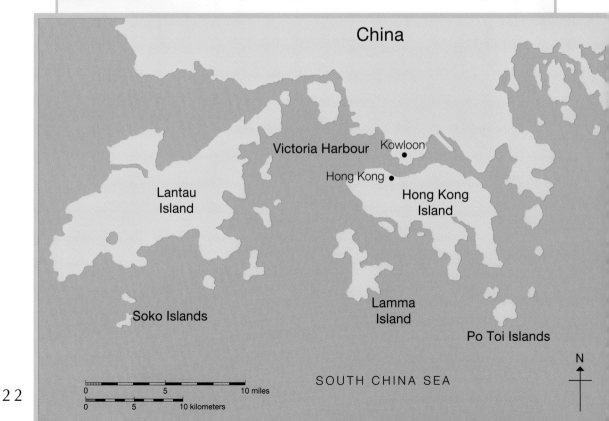

New York

The largest city in the United States, New York, is built on islands. It is made up of five sections, called boroughs. Only one of these, the Bronx, is on the mainland. The boroughs of Brooklyn and Queens are part of Long Island. Staten Island and Manhattan are separate islands. There are many smaller islands around the city, including Liberty Island in New York Bay. This is where the Statue of Liberty stands, welcoming visitors to the city. Manhattan is New York's business and entertainment center. Bridges and tunnels connect the island to the rest of the city.

● *Santa Cruz de Tenerife, in the Canary Islands, is an important deep-water port. The islands were named after the Latin for "dog" (canis), because ancient sailors saw fierce dogs there. Canary birds are named after the islands.*

The Canary Islands

The 13 islands that make up the Canary Islands form 2 of the 50 provinces of Spain, but their nearest mainland is the African country of Morocco. They were important because they provided harbors when sailing south. Christopher Columbus stopped there to take on water and supplies before sailing across the Atlantic to the New World in 1492. The islands' use has changed over the years. The Canaries have pleasant weather all year round, and today they are a very popular vacation spot.

Changing Islands

Islands change over long periods of time. **Continental** islands move further away from the **mainland.** Oceanic islands get lower when their **volcanoes** stop **erupting.** We never notice these tiny changes—but what if sea levels were to rise around the world? That would flood many coasts and have a terrible effect on low-lying islands.

Many scientists believe that ice at the North and South Poles is melting, because the worldwide temperature is rising. This is |partly due to the **greenhouse effect,** which is caused by heat-trapping gases. These allow heat through to Earth from the Sun, but trap it there, like the glass of a greenhouse. The gases we release by burning **fuel,** such as the gasoline we use to power our cars, add to this effect. It may cause a general increase in temperature, called **global warming,** which would create many problems, especially for islands.

This is one of the many islands that make up the Maldives. It has a small harbor for fishing boats and visiting yachts. The whole country has a population of about 285,000.

The Maldives

The country of the Maldives is made up of about 1,200 small **coral** islands that form a long **archipelago.** This chain of islands in the Indian Ocean is more than 466 miles (750 kilometers) long. Most of the islands are very low-lying, rising less than 6.5 feet (2 meters) above sea level. The highest point is just 79 feet (24 meters) high. Coconut palms and fruit trees grow on the islands, many of which are popular with **tourists.** Most islanders make a living from fishing and tourism. Any rise in sea level would drown some of the islands, and a big rise would cover all of them.

The Queen of the Adriatic

Venice, in northern Italy, is an island city built on about 120 **islets.** These are linked by more than 400 bridges. The city has canals instead of roads, so people travel by boat instead of by car. Its famous traditional boats are called gondolas (right). Founded in the 7th century, Venice became an important trading city, which some people called the "Queen of the Adriatic." It has many beautiful buildings and is a wonderful place for tourists to visit. The city is often flooded, however, and the floods have weakened the foundations of many buildings. This problem would be made worse by any rise in sea level.

Tourism

Islands are very popular with **tourists** because islands have lots of beaches. When tourists first come to an island, the local people generally welcome them. Tourism brings jobs and income to the islanders—but when there are too many tourists, problems can arise. Small, quiet fishing villages turn into noisy places full of hotels and restaurants. Before too long the original reasons people wanted to visit the islands are gone, and many locals have moved away.

Mediterranean islands

Many islands in the Mediterranean Sea have become very popular with tourists. These include the Spanish Balearic Islands. The Balearics are made up of four main islands, three of which have international airports. The largest island, Mallorca, is a popular destination for vacationers. It has a few very busy beach resorts, but much of the island remains undeveloped. Next comes Menorca, then Ibiza, which is well known as a fun place for young people to visit. The smallest island is Formentera, which is largely undeveloped.

In ancient times the Balearic Islands were occupied by the Vandals, Phoenicians, Romans, and many others. The islands became a Spanish province (part of Spain) in 1833. The capital of the province is Palma de Mallorca.

Menorca

Over the past 20 years, the number of visitors to Menorca has increased. The island has a lot to offer: a large, deep-water harbor and an interesting town at Mahon, the capital. It also has wonderful swimming and boating off beaches all around the island. The Menorcans realized that their island would be ruined if it lost its charm. So they stopped building high-rise hotels, and said that all new villas must be built in a traditional style.

Biosphere reserve

In 1993 UNESCO (the United Nations Educational, Scientific, and Cultural Organization) declared Menorca a Biosphere Reserve. This means it is a protected island. The Menorcans have worked hard to look after the environmental features of their island. A nature reserve was created at the eastern end of the island.

These newly built villas surround a cove on the island of Menorca.

Looking to the future

As we have seen, the world's islands change naturally over long periods of time. In recent years many islands have also changed dramatically because of the way people have treated them. Some of these changes have been good, but others have spoiled the islands' beauty. Today, nature **reserves** and national parks are often created to try and prevent unnecessary development, allowing our islands to go on changing naturally in the future.

Island Facts and Figures

The world's biggest islands

island	country	area in sq miles	area in sq km
Greenland	Denmark	840,030	2,175,600
New Guinea	Indonesia, Papua New Guinea	317,001	821,030
Borneo	Indonesia, Malaysia, Brunei	287,401	744,366
Madagascar	Madagascar	226,657	587,041
Baffin Island	Canada	183,810	476,068
Sumatra	Indonesia	182,860	473,607
Honshu	Japan	88,976	230,448
Great Britain	United Kingdom	84,186	218,041
Ellesmere Island	Canada	82,119	212,688
Victoria Island	Canada	81,930	212,198

Islands with the greatest population

island	country	population in millions
Java	Indonesia	120
Honshu	Japan	101
Great Britain	UK	56
Sumatra	Indonesia	42
Luzon	Philippines	35
Taiwan	Taiwan	22
Sri Lanka	Sri Lanka	19
Hispaniola	Haiti, Dominican Republic	16
Mindanao	Philippines	15
Madagascar	Madagascar	14

The world's highest islands

island	country	highest point	height in ft/m
New Guinea	Indonesia	Puncak Jaya	16,502 / 5,030
Hawaii	United States	Mauna Kea	13, 796 / 4,205
Borneo	Malaysia	Kinabalu	13,454 / 4,101
Taiwan	Taiwan	Yu Shan	13,113 / 3,997
Sumatra	Indonesia	Kerinci	12,487 / 3,806
Ross	Antarctica	Erebus	12,447 / 3,794
Honshu	Japan	Fuji	12,388 / 3,776
South Island	New Zealand	Cook (Aorangi)	12,316 / 3,754
Lombok	Indonesia	Rinjahi	12,224 / 3,726
Tenerife	Spain	Pico de Teide	12,198 / 3,718

Biggest islands in each continent

island	continent	country	area in sq miles	area in sq km
Greenland	N. America	Denmark	840,003	2,175,600
Borneo	Asia	Indonesia, Malaysia, Brunei	287,401	744,366
Madagascar	Africa	Madagascar	223,182	578,041
Great Britain	Europe	UK	84,186	218,041
Tierra del Fuego	S. America	Chile, Argentina	18,529	47,992
Alexander	Antarctica	–	16,679	43,200

The world's most densely populated islands

island	city/country	area in sq miles/km	pop in mills*	pop per sq mile	pop per sq km
Manhattan	New York	22 / 57	1.529	69,500	26,825
Salsette	Bombay, India	246 / 637	13	53,061	20,408
Hong Kong	China	29 / 75	1.33	47,500	17,733
Singapore	Singapore	221 / 572	3.476	15,800	6,077
Montreal	Montreal, Canada	182 / 471	1.8	9,945	3,822
Long Island	United States	1,701 / 4,406	7.4	4,350	1,679
Dakhin	Bangladesh	613 / 1,590	1.7	2,773	1,069
Java	Indonesia	51,037/132,186	120	2,351	908
Okinawa	Japan	554 / 1,434	1.2	2,170	907
Honshu	Japan	88,976 /230,448	101	1,135	438

*Only including islands with a population of more than a million.

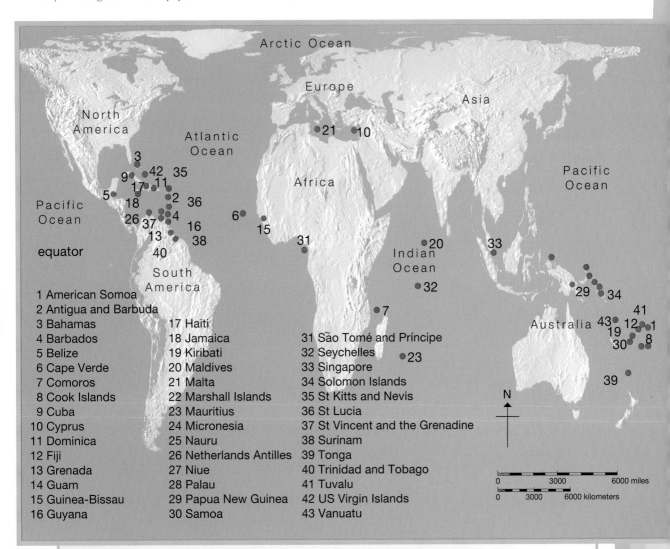

1 American Somoa
2 Antigua and Barbuda
3 Bahamas
4 Barbados
5 Belize
6 Cape Verde
7 Comoros
8 Cook Islands
9 Cuba
10 Cyprus
11 Dominica
12 Fiji
13 Grenada
14 Guam
15 Guinea-Bissau
16 Guyana
17 Haiti
18 Jamaica
19 Kiribati
20 Maldives
21 Malta
22 Marshall Islands
23 Mauritius
24 Micronesia
25 Nauru
26 Netherlands Antilles
27 Niue
28 Palau
29 Papua New Guinea
30 Samoa
31 São Tomé and Príncipe
32 Seychelles
33 Singapore
34 Solomon Islands
35 St Kitts and Nevis
36 St Lucia
37 St Vincent and the Grenadine
38 Surinam
39 Tonga
40 Trinidad and Tobago
41 Tuvalu
42 US Virgin Islands
43 Vanuatu

● This map shows the location of members of the Small Island Developing States network (SIDSnet). This group of independent islands and countries share concerns about their environment, and tries to work together within the United Nations.

Glossary

archipelago group of islands

atoll ring-shaped group of coral islands

civilization advanced culture, or a people with an advanced culture

colony large group of animals, plants, or people that live close together

continent one of the world's seven large land masses

continental relating to a large land mass (or continent)

coral tiny sea animal that forms colonies (called coral reefs) in warm, shallow waters

crust hard outer layer of Earth

descendant person who is born into a certain group of people

erupt (as a volcano) to throw out molten rock, ash, and steam with an explosion

exports goods that are sent for sale to another country

fuel material that can be used as a source of energy, such as oil

global warming rise in temperature all over the world

greenhouse effect trapping of the Sun's warmth near Earth by gases in the air

hot spot very hot layer of molten rock beneath Earth's crust; hot spots break through the earth's crust to form volcanic islands

ice age period in the past when Earth was colder and more covered in ice

ice sheet thick layer of ice covering land

inhabit to live on or in

islet small island

lagoon stretch of water surrounded and enclosed by coral islands or a reef

lava hot, molten rock that pours out of a volcano on to Earth's surface

mainland large piece of land, near which there may be smaller islands

molten melted (turned into liquid by heat)

plantation farming estate where plants like sugar cane or cotton are grown

plate huge piece of Earth's crust

predator animal that hunts and kills other animals for food

prey animal that is hunted and eaten by another

rain forest thick forest found in warm, tropical areas with heavy rainfall

reef ridge of coral near the surface of the sea

reserve area set aside to protect the animals and plants that live there

resource supply of something that can be used

sandbank deposit of sand in shallow water

seabed ground under the sea; the ocean floor

self-governing province region of a country that controls itself

species kind or type of animal or plant

territory land controlled by a country

tide rise and fall of sea level, which usually happens twice a day

tourist person visiting a place on vacation

unique one of a kind

vegetation plants; plant life

volcano opening where molten rock and gas come from deep inside Earth, often forming a mountain

Further Reading

Chambers, Catherine. *Mapping Earthforms: Islands*. Chicago: Heinemann Library, 2000.

Jennings, Terry. *Coasts and Islands*. London: Belitha Press, 1999.

Oxlade, Chris. *Earth Files: Islands*. Chicago: Heinemann Library, 2003.

Index

Aleutian Islands 8
animals and plants 10, 14–17
archipelagos 5, 8, 25
atolls 11, 15

Baffin Island 19, 28
Balearic Islands 26–27
barrier islands 12–13
biggest islands 4, 22, 28
Bikini Atoll 10
Bora-Bora 11
Borneo 4, 17, 28
British Isles 7

Canary Islands 23
continental islands 6–7, 24
continents 5, 6, 8, 15
coral islands 10–11, 15, 25
coral reefs 10, 11, 16
Crete 18
Cyclades 18–19

Delos 18

Earth's crust 6, 9
Earth's plates 6, 8

farming 21
Faroes 19
formation of an island 5, 6–9, 10, 12
Formentera 26

Galápagos Islands 15, 16
global warming 24
Greenland 4, 6, 19, 22, 28

harbors 22, 23, 27
Hatteras Island 13
Hawaiian Islands 8, 9, 19, 28
hills and mountains 6, 8, 9
Hong Kong 22, 29
Honshu 4, 28, 29

Ibiza 26
Iceland 9, 19
island arcs 8
island reserves 16, 17, 27
islets 4, 5, 9, 25

Japan 5, 28, 29

Kythnos 19

Long Island 12, 23, 29

Madagascar 5, 6, 14, 28
mainland 6, 8, 12, 22, 24
Maldives 10, 24–25, 29
Mallorca 26
Marshall Islands 10, 11, 29
Menorca 26, 27
Mont-Saint-Michel 7

New Guinea 4, 28
New York 23, 29
New Zealand 15, 16, 19, 28
oceanic islands 8, 24

Philippines 8, 17
Polynesians 19

populations 22, 28, 29

rain forests 17, 21

seabed 6, 8, 9
sea level 7, 24, 25
settlements 18–21
Shetlands 19
slavery 20
Small Island Developing States network (SIDSnet) 29
St Lucia 20–21, 29
Sumatra 5, 17, 28
Surtsey 9

Tenerife 23, 28
tidal islands 7
tides 7
tourism 5, 7, 21, 22, 23, 25, 26–27

Venice 25
Vikings 19
Virgin Islands 16, 29
volcanic islands 8, 9, 11
volcanoes 5, 8, 11, 24
voyages of exploration 18–19, 20